GIANT TORTOISES

by Jaclyn Jaycox

PEBBLE
a capstone imprint

Pebble Explore is published by Pebble, an imprint of Capstone.
1710 Roe Crest Drive
North Mankato, Minnesota 56003
www.capstonepub.com

Library of Congress Cataloging-in-Publication data is available on the Library of Congress website.
ISBN 978-1-9771-3195-9 (library binding)
ISBN 978-1-9771-3297-0 (paperback)
ISBN 978-1-9771-5430-9 (eBook PDF)

Summary: Text describes giant tortoises, including where they live, their bodies, what they do, and dangers to giant tortoises.

Image Credits
Capstone Press: (map) 6; Newscom: Tui De Roy/ Minden Pictures, 22; Shutterstock: Alberto Loyo, bottom 12, Danita Delmont, 11, David Evison, 21, Don Mammoser, 17, emirhankaramuk, 23, FOTOGRIN, Cover, Jess Kraft, 24, JMP_Traveler, top 12, Kertu, 15, Lidiya Oleandra, 18, Maridav, 26, Marisa Estivill, 27, Mathee Suwannarak, 1, 7, qoala, 14, Salty View, 28, seasoning_17, 25, Simon Marsden, 8, Tom Jastram, 5

Editorial Credits
Editor: Hank Musolf; Designer: Dina Her; Media Researcher: Morgan Walters; Production Specialist: Tori Abraham

All internet sites appearing in back matter were available and accurate when this book was sent to press.

Table of Contents

Words in **bold** are in the glossary.

Amazing Giant Tortoises

Is that big rock moving? Wait, it's not a rock. It's a giant tortoise!

Tortoises are like turtles. But tortoises live on land. They can't swim.

Giant tortoises are a type of **reptile**. There are two types of giant tortoises. They are the Galapagos and Aldabra tortoises.

Where in the World

Giant tortoises are **rare**. They live in only two places on Earth. Galapagos tortoises are found in the Galapagos Islands. These islands are near South America.

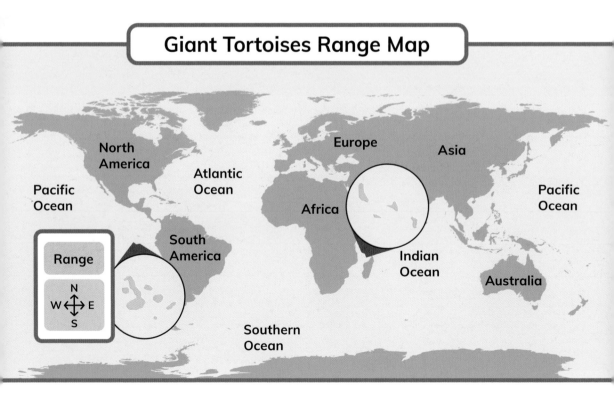

Giant Tortoises Range Map

North America

Atlantic Ocean

Pacific Ocean

South America

Range

N
W—E
S

Europe

Asia

Africa

Indian Ocean

Pacific Ocean

Australia

Southern Ocean

Aldabra tortoises live on the Seychelles Islands. They are in the Indian Ocean near Africa.

Giant tortoises live in grasslands and forests. They live in swamps and deserts too.

Giant tortoises are **cold-blooded**. If it's hot outside, they are hot. If it's cold, they are cold.

During the day, these gentle giants lay in the sun to warm up. If they get too hot, they cool off under trees or bushes. At night, it gets cold. They sleep in mud or brush to keep warm.

Gentle Giants

Giant tortoises are huge! They grow to be 4 to 5 feet (1.2 to 1.5 meters) long. Males can weigh more than 500 pounds (227 kilograms). Females weigh about half as much as males.

Giant tortoises can be brown or black. They can be dark gray too. Their legs and heads are covered with hard pieces of skin called **scales**.

Giant tortoises have two kinds of shells. A saddleback shell is curved near the neck. Tortoises with these shells can reach higher for food.

A dome shell doesn't have a curve. Tortoises with these shells can't raise their heads as high. They live where there is more food on the ground.

The shells aren't solid. They have air pockets. It makes them lighter to carry.

Giant tortoises find food with their eyes. They don't have a good sense of smell. They don't have teeth either. The edges of their mouths are bumpy and sharp. That is what they use to chew food.

These tortoises have big claws on their feet. They help them walk on rough ground. But these animals don't go anywhere fast. They walk about 0.16 mile (0.26 kilometer) per hour. Humans walk about 17 times faster.

On the Menu

Giant tortoises eat plants. They eat flowers, leaves, and grass. They eat cactuses and fruit too. They get most of their water from the plants. They also drink water if they are thirsty.

Giant tortoises can't always reach the leaves they want to eat. That's when they knock down small trees and bushes. Time to eat!

Giant tortoises' bodies break down food slowly. It can take three weeks to **digest** a meal. They can store lots of food and water in their bodies.

Many live where it is hot and dry. Sometimes food is hard to find. They can live off what is stored. They can go a year without eating or drinking!

Life of a Giant Tortoise

Giant tortoises live lazy, peaceful lives. They can sleep about 16 hours a day. The rest of the time is spent eating. When food is hard to find, they will rest and sleep all day long.

These large animals usually live alone. But they don't mind other tortoises. They come together to **mate**. They usually mate between January and May. Females then find a nesting area. A nesting area has dry, sandy ground.

Females dig holes in the ground. This is where they lay their eggs. They lay between two and 25 eggs. The eggs are about as big as tennis balls. The females cover the eggs with sand and mud. It keeps them warm and safe. The mothers leave. They do not take care of the babies.

The eggs hatch after about four months. The babies have to dig their way out. Sometimes it can take up to a month!

Babies are only about 3 inches
(7.6 centimeters) long. They grow
very slowly. It takes 40 to 50 years to
reach their full-grown size. Many don't
live past the first 10 years. Pigs, dogs,
and rats attack them.

Those that survive live very long lives. Most live to be more than 100 years old. The oldest-known giant tortoise is 187 years old!

Dangers to Giant Tortoises

The number of giant tortoises has gone down. People started building homes on the islands they live on. Animals that were new to the island came with them. Goats and cows eat the grass. There is less food for the tortoises.

Adult tortoises don't have many **predators**. Their shells keep them safe. When they are threatened, they pull their heads in.

Humans are the biggest danger to giant tortoises. It is against the law to hunt them. But some people still do.

These gentle giants are in danger of dying out. But people are trying to help. Laws have been passed to protect where they live. People help care for their eggs. They keep the young safe until they grow big enough to survive on their own.

Fast Facts

Name: giant tortoise

Habitat: grasslands, forests, swamps, dry deserts

Where in the World: Galapagos and Seychelles Islands

Food: leaves, grass, flowers, cactuses, fruit

Predators: pigs, dogs, rats, humans

Life Span: more than 100 years

Glossary

cold-blooded (KOHLD-BLUHD-id)—having a body temperature that changes with the surrounding temperature

digest (dy-GEST)—to break down food so it can be used by the body

mate (MATE)—to join with another to produce young

predator (PRED-uh-tur)—an animal that hunts other animals for food

rare (RAIR)—not often seen or found

reptile (REP-tile)—a cold-blooded animal that breathes air and has a backbone; most reptiles have scales

scale (SKALE)—one of many small, hard pieces of skin that cover an animal's body

Read More

Gagne, Tammy. *Giant Galápagos Tortoise.* Minneapolis: Abdo Publishing, 2017.

Jackson, Tom. *World's Biggest Reptiles.* Minneapolis: Hungry Tomato, 2018.

Jaycox, Jaclyn. *Reptiles: A 4D Book.* North Mankato, MN: Capstone Press, 2019.

Internet Sites

Fort Wayne Children's Zoo – Aldabra Tortoise kidszoo.org/our-animals/aldabra-tortoise/

National Geographic Kids – Galapagos Tortoise kids.nationalgeographic.com/animals/reptiles/galapagos-tortoise/

San Diego Zoo Kids – Galapagos Tortoise kids.sandiegozoo.org/animals/galapagos-tortoise

Index